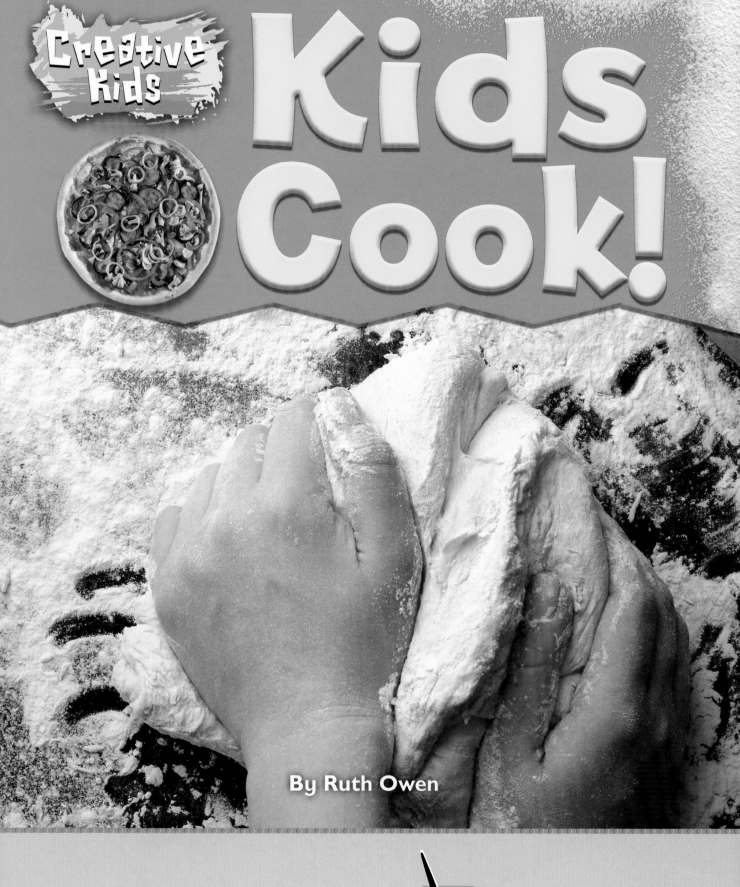

Creative Kids

Kids Cook!

By Ruth Owen

WINDMILL
BOOKS

Published in 2017 by Windmill Books,
an Imprint of Rosen Publishing
29 East 21st Street, New York, NY 10010

Copyright © 2017 by Windmill Books

First Edition

Produced for Windmill by Ruby Tuesday Books Ltd
Designer: Emma Randall

Photo Credits: Courtesy of Ruby Tuesday Books and Shutterstock

Cataloging-in-Publication Data
Names: Owen, Ruth.
Title: Kids cook! / Ruth Owen.
Description: New York : Windmill Books, 2017. | Series: Creative kids| Includes index.
Identifiers: ISBN 9781508192244 (pbk.) | ISBN 9781508192183 (library bound)
  | ISBN 9781508192060 (6 pack)
Subjects: LCSH: Cooking--Juvenile literature.
Classification: LCC TX652.5 O94 2017 | DDC 641.5'123--dc23

Manufactured in the United States of America
CPSIA Compliance Information: Batch # BS16PK: For Further Information contact
Windmill Books, New York, New York at 1-866-478-0556

Contents

Mixing bowl

Grater

Sieve

Saucepan

Cookie cutter

Oven mitt or potholder

Whisk

Muffin pan

Hand blender

Baking pan

Knife and chopping Board

Rolling pin

Wooden spoon

Get Creative in the Kitchen

It's not just fun to cook and then eat your own food. Cooking also gives you a chance to get creative! This book is packed with great ideas for easy-to-make food. The recipes don't only taste great, they also let you experiment and try out your own ideas for flavors and decorations.

Before You Get Cooking....

- Read the recipe carefully. Ask an adult for help if there's anything you don't understand.
- Always wash your hands using hot water and soap.
- Gather all the equipment and ingredients you will need.
- Make sure all your equipment and kitchen surfaces are clean.

Measure Your Ingredients Carefully

- Always take care to weigh and measure ingredients carefully. Getting a measurement wrong could affect the success of your dish.
- Kitchen scales and measuring cups and spoons are used to measure liquids and dry ingredients.

Some measuring cups hold up to two cups.

Measuring spoons are used for small quantities of ingredients, such as a teaspoon.

Kitchen scale

Some cups hold smaller quantities.

Stay Safe!

It's very important to have an adult around whenever you do any of the following cooking tasks:

- Using sharp utensils, such as knives and can openers.
- Using stovetop burners and the oven, and working with hot pots or pans.
- Operating kitchen appliances such as a mixer, blender, or food processor.

Ingredients:

- 3 cans pumpkin
- 1 large onion
- 6 carrots
- 2 stalks celery
- Bunch fresh parsley
- 1 tablespoon chopped garlic
- 3 tablespoons butter
- 2 teaspoons dried thyme
- Salt and pepper
- 1 pint (16 ounces) milk

Equipment:

- Mixing bowl
- Fork
- Knife and chopping board
- Saucepan
- Wooden spoon
- Potholder or oven mitt

Scrumptious Pumpkin Soup

The perfect way to warm up after trick-or-treating!

1 Scoop the pumpkin into a bowl. Use a fork to mash the pumpkin.

2 Peel the onion. Peel and wash the carrots, and wash the celery stalks. Then chop all three ingredients into small pieces.

Remember to ask an adult for help when you are using the knife.

3 Wash the parsley, then chop the leaves and stalks into tiny pieces. Keep chopping until you have four tablespoons of parsley.

4 Peel the papery skin from some garlic cloves. Chop into small pieces. You need enough garlic to fill a tablespoon.

Parsley leaf

Chopped parsley

Garlic bulb

Garlic clove

Peeled garlic clove

7

5 Put the butter into the saucepan. Heat and melt the butter on the stove over a low heat.

6 Add the chopped garlic, onion, carrot, and celery to the saucepan. Fry until they are tender. Stir every few seconds to keep them from burning.

7 Add the parsley and thyme to the saucepan. Also add half a teaspoon of salt and half a teaspoon of pepper. Stir to mix the ingredients.

8 Add the pumpkin, stirring so that all the ingredients are mixed thoroughly.

9 Add the milk and stir into the soup mixture.

Remember to ask an adult to keep watch while you're using the stove.

10 Now turn up the heat and bring the mixture to a boil, so it is bubbling.

11 Once the soup is boiling, turn down the heat. Put a lid on the pan and let the soup **simmer** gently for at least 10 minutes. About once a minute, give the soup a stir.

12 Your scrumptious pumpkin soup is now ready to eat!

13 When serving your soup, try decorating the soup with a swirl of cream and some crunchy pumpkin seeds. You can also sprinkle on any leftover **herbs**, such as parsley or thyme.

Ingredients:

- 5 ounces sharp cheddar cheese
- 1-inch-square chunk of Parmesan cheese
- 4 green onions
- 1 small red chili
- 2 cups plain flour
- 3 teaspoons baking powder
- 1 tablespoon sugar
- ½ teaspoon salt
- Large pinch cayenne pepper
- Large pinch mustard powder
- ½ stick butter
- 3 eggs
- 1 cup milk

Equipment:

- Grater
- Knife and chopping board
- Sieve
- Mixing bowl
- Small saucepan
- Small bowl
- Whisk
- Large metal spoon
- 12 large muffin cups
- Muffin tin
- Oven mitt or potholder

Cheesy Chili Muffins

Try partnering these muffins with your homemade pumpkin soup.

1 **Preheat** the oven to 375°F (190°C).

Ask an adult to keep watch when you're using the oven and stove.

2 Grate the cheddar cheese and Parmesan cheese, but keep separate.

3 Chop the green onions into thin slices.

Green onions

Chopped onions

Remember to ask an adult for help when you are using the grater and knife.

 4 Slice open the chili. Scrape out the seeds and throw them away. Chop the chili into tiny pieces.

Chili seeds

Don't touch your eyes when handling hot chilies!

11

5 Use the sieve to **sift** the flower into the mixing bowl.

6 Add the baking powder, sugar, salt, cayenne pepper, and mustard powder to the flour.

7 Put the butter into the saucepan. Heat and melt the butter on the stove over a low heat.

8 Break three eggs into a small bowl. Add the milk to the eggs and **whisk** together.

9 Add the warm, melted butter to the eggs and milk.

10 Pour the egg, milk, and butter mixture onto the flour in the mixing bowl.

 11 Add the grated cheddar cheese, green onions, and chili to the mixing bowl.

 12 Use a large metal spoon to fold the mixture until all the ingredients are just mixed together. If the mixture is lumpy, don't worry! This adds to the flavor and **texture**.

 13 Sit the muffin cups in the muffin pan and divide the mixture between the 12 cups.

14 Sprinkle the Parmesan cheese onto the muffins.

15 Bake the muffins for 20 to 30 minutes, or until they are golden and well risen.

2 hours

Makes **4** small pizzas

Ingredients:

For the pizza base:

- 3 cups white flour
- 1 teaspoon salt
- 0.25-ounce packet of easy bake yeast
- 2 tablespoons olive oil
- 1 cup of warm water
- Flour for dusting
- Oil for greasing baking pans

For the tomato sauce:

- 1 onion
- 2 garlic cloves
- 1 tablespoon olive oil
- ½ teaspoon salt
- 14 ounce can chopped tomatoes
- 2 heaped teaspoons tomato puree
- ½ teaspoon sugar
- 1 tablespoon dried basil
- 1 lemon
- ½ teaspoon black pepper

- Ready-grated mozzarella cheese
- Your choice of topping ingredients

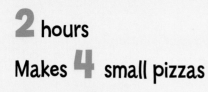

Homemade Pizzas

Don't send out for pizza when you can bake your own!

Equipment:

- Sieve
- Mixing bowl
- Chopping board
- Plastic wrap
- Knife
- Garlic crusher
- Saucepan
- Wooden spoon
- Your choice of pizza baking pans
- Paper towels
- Rolling pin

1 Sift the flour and salt into a mixing bowl.

Easy bake yeast

2 Add the yeast, olive oil, and water to the bowl.

Easy Bake Yeast

The fast, easy way to successful bread making

FOR BREAD MAKERS & HAND BAKING

3 Mix the ingredients into a ball of **dough** with your hands.

4 Sprinkle some flour onto a chopping board. Place the ball of dough onto the board and start **kneading**. Push, squeeze, and pull the dough for about eight minutes, until it's smooth and springy.

5

Place the dough back into the mixing bowl. Cover the bowl with plastic wrap and place in a warm place for an hour, or until it's doubled in size.

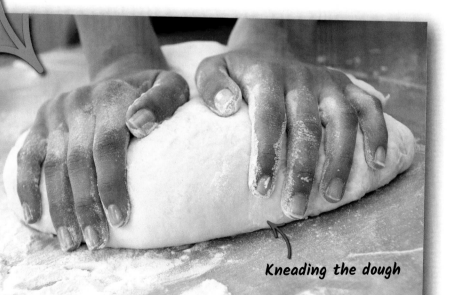

Kneading the dough

Onion

6 While the pizza dough is rising, make your tomato sauce. Chop the onion into small pieces and crush the garlic cloves.

Crushed garlic

Garlic clove

7 Pour the olive oil into a pan and heat over a medium heat.

8 Add the chopped onion and half the salt to the pan. Gently cook the onion until soft (about 5 minutes). Add the crushed garlic.

Soft, cooked onion

CHOPPED
TOMATOES
in a rich tomato juice

Tomato puree

9 Add to the pan the tomatoes, tomato puree, sugar, basil, a big squeeze of lemon juice, the remaining salt, and pepper.

Dried basil

10 Stir the sauce and leave it to gently bubble for about 10 minutes. Then set to one side.

11 Use a paper towel to smear a little olive oil over the baking pans. This will keep the pizzas from sticking to the pans.

12 Once the pizza dough has risen, place it on a flour-dusted board again and knead for about one minute. Divide the dough into four.

13 Use a rolling pin or your hands to flatten the dough. Place the pizza bases on the oiled baking pans. Leave to rise again for 15 minutes.

14 Preheat the oven to 450°F (230°C).

15 Spread your homemade tomato sauce over the pizza bases and sprinkle on some grated mozzarella cheese.

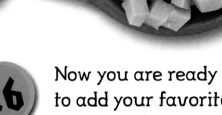

16 Now you are ready to add your favorite toppings to your pizzas.

17 Bake the pizzas for 15 to 20 minutes ...

... and ENJOY!

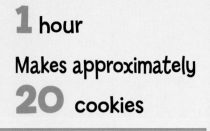

1 hour

Makes approximately **20** cookies

Ingredients:

- 12 ounces plain flour
- 2 teaspoons ground ginger
- 1 teaspoon ground cinnamon
- 1 teaspoon baking soda
- 3.5 ounces butter
- 6 ounces light, soft brown sugar
- 1 egg
- 4 tablespoons golden syrup*
- Flour for dusting
- Ready-to-use decorating icing

Equipment:

- Mixing bowl
- Sieve
- Butter knife
- Metal spoon
- Plastic wrap
- Baking pans (as required)
- Baking parchment
- Rolling pin
- Cookie cutters (your choice)
- Oven mitt or potholder
- Wire rack

Delicious Gingerbread

1 Preheat the oven to 375°F (190°C).

2 Sift the flour, ginger, cinnamon, and baking soda into a mixing bowl.

Cinnamon   Ginger

Rubbing in butter and flour

3 Cut the butter into small chunks and add to the mixing bowl.

4 Now, you are going to combine the butter with the flour using the **rubbing in** method. With your fingers, rub and squish the butter and flour together. Keep going until the mixture looks like breadcrumbs.

5 Add the sugar to the mixing bowl.

*Don't have golden syrup? You can substitute 2 tbsp. honey and 2 tbsp. corn syrup, OR 2 tbsp. + 2 tsp. molasses and 1 tbsp. + 1 tsp. light corn syrup.

6 Add an egg and the golden syrup to the mixture.

Gingerbread dough

7 Use a spoon to thoroughly mix all the ingredients together to form a dough. As the mixture gets stiffer, it's fine to dive in and use your hands!.

8 Once the dough has formed a smooth ball, wrap in plastic wrap and chill in the refrigerator for 15 minutes.

9 Cover each baking pan with a sheet of baking parchment.

10 Sprinkle some flour onto a clean surface. Unwrap the ball of gingerbread dough. Use a rolling pin to roll out the dough to ¼ inch (0.5 cm) thick.

11 Using cutters, cut out gingerbread shapes and lay them on the baking pans. Leave a space of 1 inch (2.5 cm) between each shape.

12 Bake for 10 to 15 minutes, or until the cookies feel firm but still springy when touched.

Ask an adult to keep watch when you're using the oven.

13 Carefully place the cookies onto a wire rack to cool.

14 Once cool, have fun decorating your gingerbread shapes with icing.

Chocolate Orange Cookies

1 hour

Makes approximately **12 to 15** large cookies

Ingredients:

- Butter for greasing baking pans
- 5 ounces soft butter
- 6 ounces superfine sugar
- 8 ounces plain flour
- 2 teaspoons baking powder
- Large pinch of ground cinnamon
- 3 ounces chocolate chips (your choice of dark or milk)
- 1 orange

Equipment:

- Flat baking pans
- A paper towel
- Mixing bowl
- Wooden spoon
- Sieve
- Grater
- Fork
- Oven mitt or potholder
- Wire rack

Eat warm from the oven with a big glass of milk!

1 Preheat the oven to 350°F (180°C).

2 Use a piece of paper towel to smear butter over two flat baking pans. This will keep your cookies from sticking to the pans.

3 Add the butter and sugar to a mixing bowl. Use the spoon to **beat** the butter and sugar together until it's pale and creamy.

4 Sift the flour, baking powder, and cinnamon into the mixing bowl.

5 Add the chocolate chips to the mixing bowl.

Fine side of grater

Grated orange rind

6 Wash the rind, or skin, of the orange. Use the fine side of a grater to remove the rind of the orange.

7 Squeeze two tablespoons of juice from the orange. Add the orange rind and juice to the mixing bowl.

8 Use a fork to mix all the ingredients until they form a stiff dough. Make the mixture into a ball of dough using your hands

9 Sprinkle some flour onto a chopping board or clean surface. Place the ball of dough onto the board. Use a rolling pin to roll out the dough to 1/2 inch (1 cm) thick.

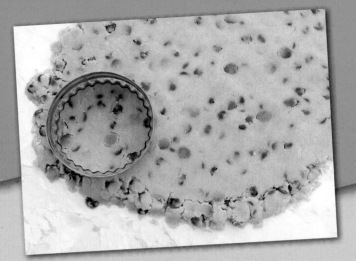

10 Cut the dough into circles with a cookie cutter. Lay the cookies on the baking pans. The dough will spread so leave a space of 1 inch (2.5 cm) between each cookie.

11 Bake the cookies for 20 to 25 minutes or until they are a pale gold color. They should feel firm but still springy.

Ask an adult to keep watch when you're using the oven.

12 Sprinkle the cookies with a little sugar. Then transfer the cookies to a wire rack to cool.

27

Ingredients:

- 2 cups strawberries

- 3 medium-sized bananas

- ½ cup thick, Greek yogurt

- 4 tablespoons honey

- 1 tablespoon lemon juice

Equipment:

- Knife and chopping board

- Freezer bag

- Mixing bowl

- Hand blender

- Freezer container

Super Fruity Ice Cream

1 Wash the strawberries and remove their stalks. Chop the strawberries into quarters.

2 Peel and slice the bananas.

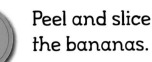

Remember to ask an adult for help when you are using a knife.

3 Put the fruit into a freezer bag and freeze for several hours, or overnight.

4 Place the frozen fruit in a mixing bowl.

5 Add the yogurt, honey, and lemon juice to the mixing bowl.

6 Use a hand blender to blend the mixture until it's smooth.

7 If you want a soft-serve texture, eat the ice cream immediately. Or pour into a freezer container and freeze for three to four hours before serving.

Try out this recipe with other fruits, such as raspberries, blackberries, blueberries, peaches, and mango.

Glossary

beat
To stir and mix at high speed to produce a smooth mixture. Beating can be done with equipment such as a spoon, fork, whisk, or food processor.

dough
A thick mixture of flour and other ingredients, including liquids such as water or milk, used for making baked goods such as bread, pizza, and cookies. Dough should be firm so it can be formed into shapes.

herbs
Plants that usually have a strong but pleasant smell and taste. They are used for adding flavor to food.

knead
To blend ingredients together to form dough, by squeezing, pushing, and pulling, using hands or a food processor.

preheat
To heat an oven to a necessary temperature before cooking.

rub in
To blend butter and flour by rubbing and squeezing it together with the fingers.

sift
To gently shake a dry ingredient, such as flour, through a sieve to break up any lumps.

simmer
To cook in a liquid on a low heat so the liquid is gently bubbling but is not boiling.

texture
How an object or substance feels to the touch or in the mouth. For example, rough, smooth, sticky, or crunchy.

whisk
To beat ingredients with a fork, whisk, or food processor. Whisking adds air and can make a mixture fluffier. It can also stiffen a liquid, such as cream, to make it thicker.

Websites

For web resources related to the subject of this book, go to: **www.windmillbooks.com/weblinks** and select this book's title.

Index